AF326595

ADVENTURES OF THE F.1 RACING RABBITS RACE

Written by Paul Macdonald
Illustrated by Pavel Goldaev

First published 2017

Email: paulmac72@bigpond.com

Manufactured in the United States of America

Written by Paul Macdonald
Illustrated by Pavel Goldaev

Dedicated to my beautiful girl and our two beautiful boys.

It's the beginning of the F.1 racing rabbits season and we are off to the beautiful Albert Park racing circuit in sunny Melbourne Australia.

Here comes the racing rabbits ready to race on the main straight on a warm summer's day.

A race official rabbit waves the green flag and the racing rabbits are off in a puff of smoke.

The racing rabbits fight for the lead in the exciting race.

Oh no, racing rabbit Vettel has crashed into racing rabbit Hamilton who doesn't look happy at all.

The crowd cheers as rabbit racer Stacey Speeds roars into the pits for a tire change.

The rabbits in the crowd are having a wonderful time drinking milk shakes and eating hot chips.

Racing rabbit Ricciardo has passed the leader
racing rabbit Alonso with one lap to go.

The race official waves his chequered flag again
as the leader racing rabbit Ricciardo crosses the
finish line waving to the crowd.

The first three finishing racing rabbits stand on top of the podium with big smiles on their faces as they hold up their winning trophies!

Who will win the next race between the racing rabbits? We will have to wait and see won't we?

The next race the F.1 racing rabbits will be off to the wonderful Monaco Grand Prix racing circuit which should be a very exciting race indeed!

Please check out our website at:

http://paulandsonspublishing.my-free.website/